To: my childre..

MW01444005

Hazel's ABC's Of Halloween

Written and Illustrated By Amy Horikami

Apple bobbing is such a tasty treat.

Bats

fly up to the moon as they screech.

Cauldrons full of Candy give

this Cat a sigh.

Quiet in the **Dungeon!**
For the **Dragon** is near. Don't stir
him from his slumber.
I have warned you, my dear.

Eerie **E**yes are glaring at ME!

Franky, my Frankenstein Friend, and I being silly.

Ghost are just Grandmas

having a spooky good time.

Haunted Houses

are **Impeccably** scary!

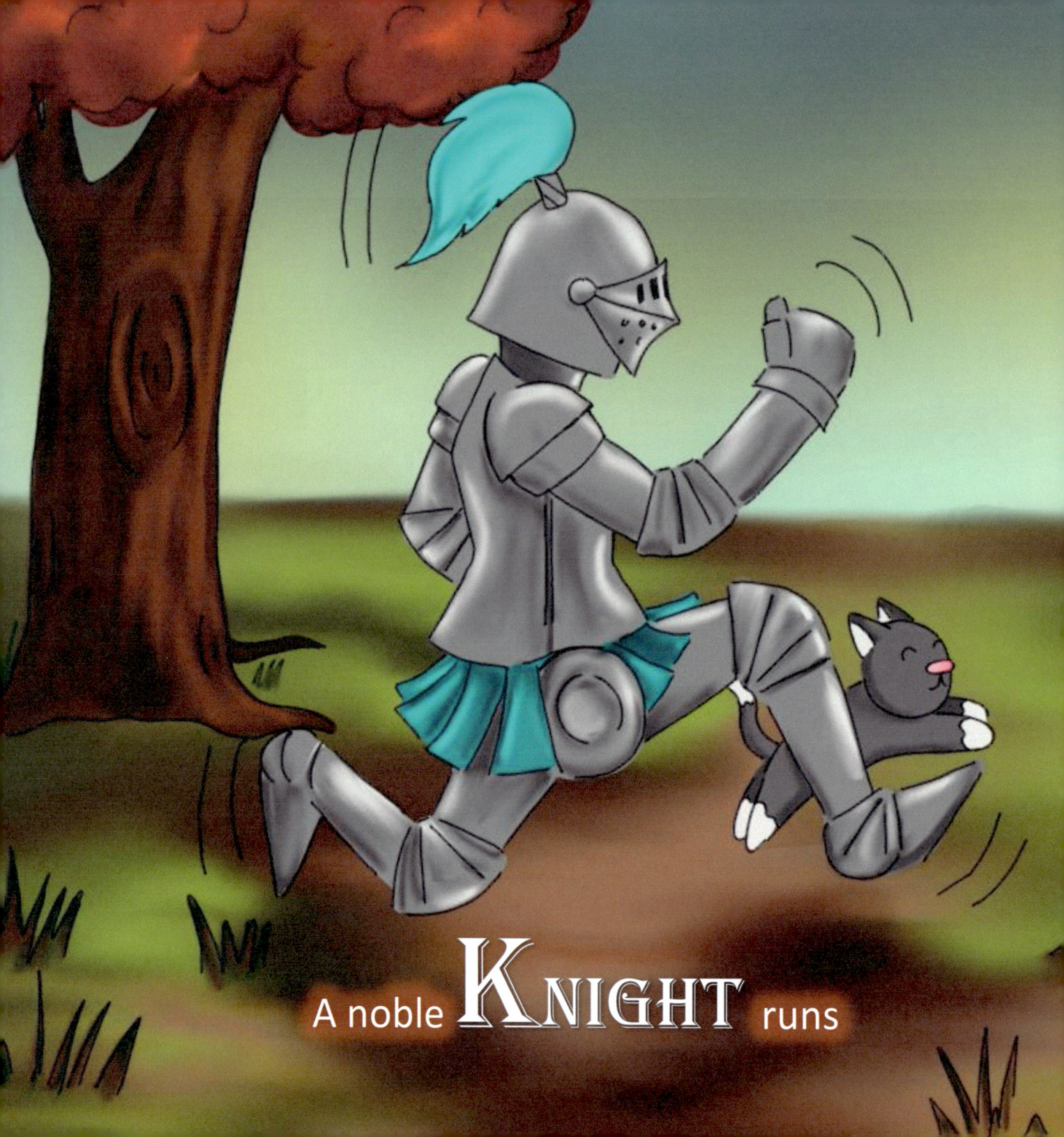

A noble KNIGHT runs

Nighttime is scary

as **O**wls watch from the trees.
Their large yellow eyes
frightening me!

Trick-or-Treating from door to door.
Candy at midnight!
Who could ask for more!

Up, up, up we GO!
Into the moonlight our silhouettes glow.

Vampire Weddings are a sight to see.
A haunted love for Eternity.

eXtra candy is so Yummy.
We even share with Zina Zombie

THE END.

Hazel's
ABC's
of
HALLOWEEN

Written and Illustrated By Amy Horikami

Made in the USA
Columbia, SC
03 May 2025

57375072R00015